A Personal Apocalypse

Morgan Bailey

BookLeaf Publishing

Presentation by *BookLeaf Publishing*

Web: www.bookleafpub.com

E-mail: info@bookleafpub.com

ISBN: 9789357445818

First edition 2022

DEDICATION

For Ash. And also for those who gave a purpose to this.

One

I showered today and realized I was washing the last of you away. the last kisses left on my face, the last time you would hold me in your arms, followed my shampoo down the drain. I tried to wash away the hopes of you coming back and deciding that you want me I tried to wash away the last words you said, that have been repeating since they came out of your mouth. but I'm still stuck with this fantasy in my head that you care and you'll come back or I'll be able to fix it.   if only I could wash away the thought of you forever.

Two

the last time I sat here was with you,
on the smallest step off the porch in my backyard,
you grabbed my hand in yours and told me you loved me.
so much has changed since then.
I fondly recall now how I couldn't focus on anything but your eyes,
the chill in the air brought me closer to you.
this time around the crickets fill the emptiness,
that has been surrounding me since you left.
I let myself shiver,
and wonder if you were here,
how different things would be.

Three

I find myself searching for remnants of you.
pieces of the person I thought I understood
left over from the storm that you so carelessly
created.
castaway fragments of an identity I could once
correctly perceive
but now struggle to pick apart.
and as I search for these omitted components of
someone I cherished,
my hopelessness grows more and more.
because how will I ever repair the misplaced
shape my soul has morphed into,
when I cannot seem to rehabilitate the idea I
have of you in my head,
to fit this new persona you have constructed.
and as the nights grow longer, and days shorten,
perhaps those forgotten pieces will materialize.
or perhaps it is all a tragic and solemn endeavor
that ends with me forgetting who you were.

Four

you used to call me beautiful.
so much it never felt like a compliment. almost a need rather than a want.
it became fully expected rather than used as flattery.
comparisons between my earthly body and earthly beauty were not uncommon,
and remarks on what you saw in me solely customary.

now I struggle to remember how you saw delicacy in my flaws.
instead, your words are filled with incantations of what I lack.
your eyes have lost the old look of loving intoxication,
presently they see what there is too much of,
what could be adjusted or covered.

and where you once found beauty in my words,
exclusively remorse remains.

Five

I still remember the way your hand felt wrapped
around mine as we jumped into the water
loose at first, just encouragement.
but then tighter as you saw how nervous I was
and then firm enough to turn my hand white
because you thought about what might happen
and we jumped fell farther our grip loosened
and farther
looser
farther
looser
until finally we hit the water the impact was hard
and frightening and all at once
you let go.

Six

often I would let my brain have runaway
thoughts,
imagining scenarios in order to bring about
peace.
I would create false realities that seem
achievable to me,
but would look impossible to you.
one realistic element turned into a daydream of
delusion.
always ending in bitter disappointment.
with no one to blame but myself.
you would materialize, reappear, explain your
feelings of anguish about what you had done to
me.
and fulfill those empty promises you had once
made.
I saw that potential in you,
chose not to ignore what could be.
and began to anticipate futures that would never
come.

Seven

emotional permanence: the idea that even with a lack of proof, emotions continue to exist. a feeling of warmth emerging from reminiscent memories. I lose any sense of emotional permanence the second I begin to think about you. about what happened, about all of those valuable words, now meaningless in comparison to the path you chose. supposed everlasting affection is dismissed as soon as you walk away. and doubt fills me as you repeat those same promises to another.

Eight

driving on an interstate at sunset brings about a
funny lesson.
as passengers turn their heads to watch the day
come to a close,
the driver is forced to keep focus ahead.
a kind of torture derived from responsibility.
because although the driver should be allowed to
witness those crepuscular rays, fixating upon the
right side lane is all they can do.
I find myself as the driver when comparing this
situation to ours.
because it feels right with you, being held in
your arms is better for mending my soul than
any other vices.
glancing over to witness a beautiful array of
colors seems to be my instinctual reaction
withyou as the sunset.
but as I stare in wonder and amazement,
I become more aware of the danger that a human
sunset possesses.
and wish to myself that we lived in a fair world.
where the driver could take in every ounce of
peace that comes along with your dusk, instead
of facing beautifully tragic fatality.

Nine

I'll fix it.
just tell me what to change.
explain to me how to adjust my viewpoint to fit
within your outlook on the world.
give me a guide on what I lack.
point out every little flaw.
I promise I'll make the change.
if it makes you happy,
I'll erase the person I've become,
the one I've grown into,
that the universe has crafted,
she can disappear if it enhances how you see me.
I will omit the parts of my soul I have become so
attached to,
if it means another prospect at flourishing for
you.

but I must ask myself: why do I not fit within the mold you have created? how have I become inferior due to a deficiency in what you deem important? and once I cut away any remaining virtues of who I once was, what will there be left?

Ten

I cannot sleep. I cannot allow myself to feel that rest. as exhaustion spreads throughout my body, I continue to feel tortured. and so I lie there, still and shaking. my thoughts become a buzz of overwhelming noise, I am enchanted by the repetition of my shortcomings, mesmerized by the mistakes I made. wondering how I could allow myself to behave this way, and answering the questions I have asked myself for so long, of why I seem to be insufferable.

this sleep-deprived version of myself always finds those answers. the lull of anxiety is familiar but so uncomfortable. and once my brainwork at last comes to a close, my sleep is no escape from my self-imposed distress.

Eleven

the potential is what allows me to push forward.
the thought of what could be without limitations
of reality.
looking around and realizing,
I could make something out of this.
I could make something out of us.

Twelve

exposure to your heart is frightening.
having any amount of power over what comes
for your future seems too big a responsibility.
but I would accept that burden any day if it
meant gaining insight into who you are.
because that is what I have sought after,
the vulnerability of your openness leading to
my defenselessness seems safe.

Thirteen

I pray for you every night.
even during those times where I doubt in God.
and when that doesn't seem to work,
I wish on every single star.
I spend birthday candle wishes on the thought of you,
waste away dandelions in hopes of a trade,
my breath for a moment of being yours again.
and in those prayers, I barter with God.
to bring you the happiness you've been searching for,
to fill your days with the self-fulfillment I know you crave.
I pray you'll find yourself again,
and see the future through hopeful eyes,
I pray someday you'll be able to see yourself,
as the capable, alluring person you are.
and after I beg God to bring you joy again,
I ask Him if maybe I could be a part of that optimistic future.
because although my prayers turn selfish, I still believe it's us in the end.

Fourteen

five months and five days.
five months and five days,
that's how long it took to fall apart.
for the plot to begin,
and then come to a final curtain call.
for all the streetlights to turn green,
and then change back to red.
for the leaves to fall away,
and then grow back new.
five months and five days should feel like growing,
but since you're gone it feels like shrinking.
I wish I knew what I did wrong,
I wish I knew what to apologize for,
I wish I could live in those five months and five days forever.
five months and five days;
that's the time it took for you to fall out of love.
that's the time it took for me to become alone again.

Fifteen

I'm sitting in my bed
7:12 am
I see a post you liked
it reminded me of something that should remind
you of me
I wonder if you thought of me
maybe you meant to send it my way
maybe you didn't mean to kiss them
maybe you meant to come to my place on Friday
maybe we're just a happy collection of maybes
or maybe it would always work out this way.

Sixteen

I thought I was shaking because of the cold.
I thought I was shaking as a simple reaction to the weather.
for so long I believed that.
and now I sit here,
shaking,
uncontrollably,
no way to escape it.
the anxiety makes its way down my body,
starting with a headache and then trouble breathing and then pain in my stomach and then my hands and feet begin to sweat.
and all I can think,
is how I need you here,
to hold me,
tell me how to fix myself,
help me out of this place,
please I beg you.
but I don't know where you are.

Seventeen

we listened to bon iver while I drove you home,
that final time.
I had a feeling it would be the end,
but I didn't say goodbye.
now you're too far gone,
nothing but a memory
and impressions on my skin
and the smell lingering on my clothes
and the emptiness I feel.
and those small things you left behind,
insignificant to you,
but they make up my whole world.
now I listen to bon iver as I pass that road,
and can never muster up a sufficient goodbye.

Eighteen

I never thought I'd hold a hand,
that didn't make me full of fear.
but your hand,
delicate fingers and scars from the cold.
wraps me in a hug that doesn't suffocate but
guides me.
and with your hand in mine,
I feel overwhelming safety.

Nineteen

at last I have become accustomed to this natural progression,
where we no longer spend time anticipating our futures together.
and instead I use that time,
to dream of what there is to come for me.
because we were built on a foundation of anxieties,
seeking each other out through self-destruction.

Twenty

it's raining again,
and I'm thinking of you.
of how the showers hurt before you,
but the stinging from hot water increased with
your absence.
the same rainfall that used to drench us,
as we laughed together laying in the street,
serves as a reminder of my solitude.   rain should
symbolize new starts, washing the slate clean,
bringing new life to us all drop by drop. so I will
use this downpour as a fresh beginning for
myself, rather than an excuse to reminisce on
those nights, where we pulled over in the storm
to avoid getting soaked, but also to avoid the
eventual solemn thunderstorms we would face.

Twenty-one

perishable happiness is still happiness. that is why I feel comfortable with the knowledge that this moment is limited. the obsession I have with my world at this point in time is dream-like. I am overtaken by the relief of instability. this joy may not be everlasting, but experiencing this harmony gives me something to look back on. something to explain why we allow ourselves to suffer. temporary bliss along with the awareness of how short-lived it can be, separates those who seek peace of mind, from those who will live a life with perfect memories.

www.ingramcontent.com/pod-product-compliance
Lightning Source LLC
Chambersburg PA
CBHW051719130826
49812CB00034B/1258
9789357445818